Contents

NOAH'S ARK : IS THE VESSEL MENTIONED IN THE GENESIS FLOOD STORY

GOLU KUMAR

ONE

In "the good place" of the Frankfort _Judengasse on a summer's day near the end of the first quarter of the nineteenth century after Christ, Peloni strolled and thought. His black eyes burned within, and he occasionally stopped and looked to be studying the carvings on the toppled tombstones or the cut dragons, shields, and stars. However, he was seeing the tragedy of Jewish existence rather than the tragedy of Jewish death.

Because "the good place" was where people died.

Here alone in Frankfort--in this shut-in bit of the shut-in Jew street--was true peace for Israel. The rest of the Jew street offered comparative tranquillity even for the living; yet when, ninety years before Peloni was born, the great fire had raged therein, the inhabitants had locked the Ghetto-gate against the Christians, less fearful of the ravaging flames than of their fellow-citizens. Even today, if he ventured outside the _Judengasse_, Peloni must tread delicately. The foot-path was not for him: he must plod on the dusty road, with all the other beasts. In some places, the very road was too holy for him, and any passer-by might snatch off his hat in punishment for his breaking bounds. The ragged street urchin or the staggering drunkard might cry to him "_' Jud,' much mores_: Jew, mind your manners."

Some ten years ago the Frankfort Ghetto had been verbally abolished by a civilized archduke, caught up in the wave of Napoleonic toleration. Pelosi had shared in the exultation of the Jews at the final dissipation of the long night of mediævalism. He had written a Hebrew poem on it, brilliantly rhymed, congested with apt quotations from the Bible and Talmud, the whole making an acrostic upon the name of the enlightened Karl Theodor von Dalberg. Henceforth Israel would take his place among the peoples, honor on his brow, love in his heart, manhood in his limbs. A gracious letter of acknowledgment from the archduke was displayed in the window of Peloni's little bookselling establishment, amid the door-amulets, phylacteries, praying shawls, Purim scrolls, and Hebrew volumes.

But now the prince had been ousted, Napoleon was dead, everywhere the Ghetto-gates was locked again, and the Poem lay stacked on the remainder shelves. In vain had the grateful Jews hastened to fight for the Fatherland, tendered it body and soul. Poor little curly-haired Peloni had been attacked in the streets as an alien that very morning. Roysterers had raised the old cry of "Hep! Hep!"--fatal, immemorial cry, ghastly heritage of the Crusades. Century after century that cry had gone echoing through Europe. Century after century the Jews thought they had lived it down, bought it down, died it down. But no! it rose again, buoyant, menacing, irresponsible. Ah, what a fool he had been to hope! There was no hope.

Rarely, indeed, since the Dark Ages had persecution flaunted itself so openly. Riots and massacres were breaking out all over Germany, and in his Ghetto, Peloni had seen sights that had turned his patriotism to gall and crushed his trust in the Christian, his beautiful bubble-dreams of the Millennium. Rothschild himself, whose house in the

Judengasse with the sign of the red shield had been the center of the attack, was well-nigh unable to maintain his position in the town. And these local successes inflamed the Jew-haters everywhere. "Let the children of Israel be sold to the English," recommended a popular pamphlet of the period, "who could employ them in their Indian plantations instead of the blacks. The best plan would be to purge the land entirely of this vermin, either by exterminating them, or, as Pharaoh, and the people of Meiningen, Würzburg, and Frankfort did, by driving them from the country."

"Oh, God!" thought Peloni, as his mind ran over the long chain from Pharaoh to Frankfort. "Evermore to wander, stoned and derided! Thou hast set a mark on his forehead, but his punishment is greater than he can bear."

The dead lay all around him, one upon another, new red stones shouldering aside the gray stones that told to boot off the death of the centuries. And the pressure of all this struggle for death-room had raised the earth higher than the adjacent paths. He thought of how these dead had always come here; even in their lifetime, when the enemy raged outside. Here they had put the women and children and gone back to the synagogue to pray. Ah, the cowards! always oscillating betwixt cemetery and synagogue, why did they not live, why did they not fight? Yes, but they had fought,--fought for Germany, and this was Germany's reply.

But could they not fight for themselves then, with money, with the sinews of war, if not with the weapons; with gold, if not with steel? could they not join financial forces all through the world? But no! There was no such solidarity as the Christians dreamed. And they were too mixed up with the European world to dream of self-concentration. Even while the Frankfort Rothschild's house was surrounded by rioters, the Paris Rothschild was giving a ball to the _élite_ of diplomatic society.

No! The synagogue and the cemetery were all that existed, which proved the old Jews correct.

But was the synagogue even there? That was also deceased. The living faith, the vivid realization of Israel's hope, which had made the Dark Ages bearable and even luminous, was now only to be found among fanatics whose blatant ignorance and ferocious clinging to the obsolete form and dead letter counterbalanced the poetry and sublimity of their persistence. Pelosi believed that his poems would have been incorporated into the liturgy in the Middle Ages. Because, like all living things, when the ritual and the religion were alive, they received and expended energy. However, the synagogue of today was abandoned.

There was only the cemetery left.

Juliane, Derrek! Jew, perish like a lion.

Yes, what else could be done? He told himself with whimsical agony that he was not even a Rothschild, but only a poor poet who was unread, unknown, and unhealthy; a shadow who only lived to suffer; a set of heartstrings across which every wind that blew made poignant, passionate music; a lamentation personified; a voice of weeping in the wilderness; a bubble blown of tears; a dream; a nobody; in short, Peloni!

He was drawn to the past generations. He stumbled upon a tomb while sobbing passionately.

part 2

When Peloni entered the _Judengasse again, there appeared to be an unanticipated commotion. Was a new riot on the horizon? He reflected as he moved through the one-way street lined with three-story frame homes, many of which had gables and were all distinguished by odd symbols and designs, such as the Red Shield (_Rothschild_), the Bear, the Lion, the Garlic, or the Garlic.

Outside the synagogue loitered a crowd, and as he drew near he perceived that there was a long Proclamation in a couple of folio sheets nailed on the door. It was doubtless this which was being discussed by the little groups he had already noted. About the synagogue door, the throng was so thick that he could not get near enough to read it himself. But fortunately, one was engaged in reading it aloud for the benefit of those on the outskirts.

"Therefore I, Mordecai Manuel Noah, Citizen of the United States of America, late Consul of said States to the City and Kingdom of Tunis, High Sheriff of New York, Counselor-at-Law, and by the Grace of God Governor and Judge of Israel, have issued this my proclamation," the declaration said.

The reading was cut short by a dwarfish individual in the audience laughing mockingly. Father Noah, resurrect yourself! Even when not performing for a living, the _Possemacher_, or wedding-jester, was not stingy with his wit.

A more serious voice sneered, "A foreigner—an American!" "Who installed him as Israel's ruler?"

That is what the evil Israelite asked Moses, I tell you! Pelosi screamed out with astonished wonder.

Others yelled, "Nun, nun! Go on!"

"'Announcing to the Jews throughout the world, that an asylum is prepared and hereby offered to them, where they can enjoy that Peace, Comfort, and Happiness which have been denied them through the intolerance and misgovernment of former ages. Asylum in a free and powerful country, where ample protection is secured to their persons, their property, and religious rights; an asylum in a country remarkable for its vast resources, the richness of its soil, and the salubrity of its climate; where the industry is encouraged, education promoted, and good faith rewarded. "A land of Milk and Honey," where Israel may repose in Peace, under his "Vine and Fig tree," and where our People may so familiarize themselves with the science of government and the lights of learning and civilization, as may qualify them for that great and final Restoration to their ancient heritage, which the times so powerfully indicate.'"

The crowd had become more focused. Pelosi had a deathly pallor. What was this magnificent gift that had so abruptly descended from the unmoving skies that his despondency had challenged?

However, the _Possemacher_ caught the action. "Father Noah is wasted once more!"

A loud laugh jolted the audience. Peloni, though, sank his nails into his hands. He yelled hoarsely, "Read on! Read on!"

The largest state in the American Union, New York, has the Place of Refuge, and Grand Island is the location I welcome my dear People from all over the world to.

Pelosi inhaled deeply. Now, his expression had completely reversed, and was flushed with joy.

The Possemacher exclaimed dryly, "Noah's Ark!" and caused his audience to sway madly.

Pelosi screamed, "For God's sake, brethren! "It is not a joke. Have you already forgotten that we are but animals here?"

The _Possemacher_ said, "And they went in two by two, the clean beasts, and the unclean beasts."

Some in the audience shouted, "Hush, hush, let us hear!"

"I have made up my mind to build the State of Ararat here."

What did I say, I wonder? Pelosi was startled by the jubilant Possemacher's shout.

The crowd exclaimed, "Ha! ha! ha!" Ararat is where Noah's Ark is resting. Even a moron could see that.

Pelosi was momentarily surprised.

He questioned his neighbors, "But why shouldn't the location of Israel's Ark of Refuge be named Ararat?"

If only he wasn't named Noah, they exclaimed.

He said, "That makes it much more suitable."

But the moniker "Noah's Ark" is lethal. However, the reader only continued to an audience that was enthralled by a sense of Arabian Nights' dream. However, the detailed account of this Grand Island's splendors and the poetic passages about the Century of Right and the ancient Oracles brought Peloni's passion back to a fever pitch.

The reader finally grew fatigued and remarked, "It's too long.

Pelosi moved quickly to begin the task. He was further elevated by the first sentence.

"'In God's name, I revive, renew, and reëstablish the government of the Jewish Nation, under the auspices and protection of the Constitution and the Laws of the United States, confirming and perpetuating all our Rights and Privileges, our Name, our Rank, and our Power among the nations of the Earth, as they existed and were recognized under the government of the Judges of Israel.'" Pelosi's voice shook with fervor. As he began the next sentence, "'It is my will,'" he stretched out his hand with an involuntary regal gesture. The spirit of Noah was entering into him, and he felt almost as if it was he who was re-creating the Jewish nation--"'It is my will that a Census of the Jews throughout the world be taken, that those who are well treated and wish to remain in their respective countries shall aid those who wish to go; that those who are in military service shall until further orders remain true and loyal to their rulers.

"'I order'" "That a strict Neutrality be maintained in the impending battle between Greece and Turkey," read Peloni with broad splendor, his poet's soul resonating with the other royal dreamers across the great Atlantic.

"I abrogate permanently"

"Polygamy among the Jews," said Peloni as his palm swept the air.

However, where is polygamy? the _Possemacher_ was cut off.

Pelosi harshly said, "'As it is still practiced in Africa and Asia.'"

The marriage jester yelled, "I'm gone at once for Africa and Asia!" while feigning to run. "Good trade there for me."

"You'll find better business in America," said Peloni scathingly. "For do not all our Austrian young men fly thither to marry, seeing that at home only the eldest son may found a family? A pretty fatherland indeed to be a citizen of--a step-fatherland. Listen, on the contrary, to the noble tolerance of the Jew. 'Christians are freely invited.'"

"Ah! Who will go, do you know?" a zealot with a thin face broke in. "The\smissionaries."

Pelosi quickly continued: "The Karaites and Samaritans are also welcome in Ararat. All are welcome, including our brothers in Cochin, China, and the sect on the Malabar coast. The Black Jews of India and Africa are also welcome."

A big Jewish man laughed, "Ha! ha! ha!" "Thus, we must coexist with black people.
This prank must end now!"

A Capitation-tax on every Jew of Three Silver Shekels Per Annum, Peloni said solemnly.

Ah, let's get to it now. then the crowd let up a roar. Not a bad business, eh? they winked, too. This Noah is not an idiot.

Pelosi's blood boiled. "Do you believe everybody is like yourselves?" he cried. "Listen!"

"'I do appoint the first day of next Adar for a Thanksgiving Day to the God of Israel, for His divine protection and the fulfillment of His promises to the House of Israel. I recommend Peace and Union among ourselves, Charity and Good-will to all, Toleration and Liberality toward our Brethren of all Religions--'"

The zealot said, "Didn't I mention a missionary in disguise?"

"I humbly entreat to be remembered in your prayers and earnestly do I enjoin you to "keep the charge of the Holy God," to walk in His ways, to keep His Statutes and His Commandments, and His Judgments and Testimonies, as written in the Laws of Moses; "that thou mayest prosper in all thy doest and whithersoever thou turnest thyself," Pelosi said in closing.

Given in the State of New York on February 2, 1955, the fifty-first year of American independence, under our hand and seal.

Pelosi's efforts to organize a company of pilgrims to the New Jerusalem brought him only heartache. The very rabbi who had good-naturedly consented to circulate the fantastic foreigner's invitation tapped his forehead significantly: "A visionary! of good intentions, doubtless, but still--a visionary. Besides, according to our dogmas, God alone knows the epoch of the Israelitish restoration; He alone will make it known to the whole universe, by signs entirely unequivocal; and every attempt on our part to reassemble with any political, national design, is forbidden as an act of high treason against the Divine Majesty. Mr. Noah has doubtless forgotten that the Israelites, faithful to the principles of their belief, are too much attached to the countries where they dwell, and devoted to the governments under which they enjoy liberty and protection, not to treat as a mere jest the chimerical consulate of a pseudo-restorer."

The pals of Peloni informed him, "Noah's a maniac, and you're an infant."

He responded, "The gift of prophecy has been restricted to infants and idiots since the destruction of the Temple."

They cautioned him, "You are leaving up a respectable livelihood." You're casting it into the Atlantic, I see.

"Cast thy bread upon the rivers, and thou shalt get it after many days."

But in the interim?

The saying "Man does not survive by bread alone"

"as you see fit. But please don't ask us to leave our cozy house."

"Homey and cozy!" Pelosi became almost hysterical as he recalled their woes.

"Persecution?" They gave a shoulder shrug. It only happens occasionally, like a snowstorm, and we have to crawl through it.

"That's exactly it—the dearth of manliness—the toxic environment!"

"Bah! We are denied equal rights by the "Goyim" because they recognize our superior status. Let's avoid jumping from one inferno to another."

Pelosi set off for New York on his own.

part 3

Not even another pilgrim was aboard the ferry, which left him feeling somewhat let down.
There was one Jew, it's true, but his destination across these waste seas was New York's business paradise, and he had never heard of Noah's Ark. Due to his hazy understanding of Grand Island's potential for commerce, Peloni's panegyric of the island was ineffective. He spent his downtime in the sailing ship honing his English, which he had long mastered through reading.

In New York, Peloni's hopes revived. Major Noah--for it appeared he was an officer of militia likewise--was in everybody's mouth. Editor of the _National Advocate_, the leading organ of the Bucktails, or Tammany party, a journalist whose clever sallies and humorous paragraphs were widely enjoyed, an author of excellent "Travels," a playwright of the first distinction, whose patriotic dramas were always given on the Fourth of July, a critic regarded as Sir Oracle, a politician, lawyer, and man of the world, a wit, the gay center of every gathering--surely in this lion of New York, who was also the Lion of David, Israel had at last found a deliverer. They called him madman down in Frankfort, did they? Well, let them come here and see.

He wrote home to the scoffers of the _Judengasse_ all the information about the great man that was in the very air of the American city, though the man himself he had only as yet corresponded with. He told the famous story of how when Noah was canvassing for the office of High Sheriff of New York, it was urged that no Jew should be put into an office where he might have to hang a Christian, to which Noah had retorted wittily, "Pretty Christian, to have to be hanged!" "And you all fancied 'Father Noah' would fall to pieces before the _Possemacher's_ wit!" Pelosi commented with vengeful satisfaction. "I rejoice to say that Noah will never have anything to do with a _Possemacher_, for he is President of the Old Bachelors' Club, the members of which are pledged never to marry." He told of Noah's adventurous career: of how when he was a mere boy clerk in the auditor's office of his native Philadelphia, Congress had voted him a hundred dollars for his precocious preparation of the actuary tables for the eight-per-cent loan; of the three duels at Charleston, in which he had vindicated at once the courage of the Jew and the policy of American resistance to Great Britain; of his consulate in Tunis, his capture at sea by the British fleet during the war, his release on parole that enabled him to travel about England; of his genius for letters--a very David in Israel; of his generosity to hundreds of strugglers; of his quixotic disdain of money; of his impoverishing himself by paying two hundred thousand dollars of other people's debts as the price of his impulsive shrieval action in throwing open the doors of the Debtor's Jail when yellow fever broke out within. "Yes," wrote Peloni exultantly, "in New York they talk no more of Shylock. And with all the temptations to Christian fellowship or Pagan free-living, a pillar of the synagogue,--nay, Israel's one hope in all the world!"

It was a wonderful moment when Peloni, at last invited to call on the Judge of Israel, palpitated on the threshold of his study and gazed blinkingly at the great man enthroned before his writing table amid elegant vistas of books and paintings. What a noble poetic vision it seemed to him: the broad brow, with the tumbled hair; the long, delicate-featured face tapering to a narrow chin environed with whiskers, but clean of beard or even of mustache so that the mobile, sensitive mouth was laid bare. Pelosi's glance also took in a handsome black coat, with a decoration on the lapel, a high-peaked collar, a black puffy bow, a frilled shirt, and a very broad jeweled cuff over a white, long-fingered hand, that held a tall quill with a great breadth of a feather.

The Governor of Israel said, waving his quill, "Ah, come in." "You represent Frankfort as Peloni."

Come 3,000 kilometers to kiss the hem of your clothing.

Noah gave the attention his consent. He remarked sarcastically, "I thank you for your Hebrew poem in honor of my enterprise. "Hebrew is good because it connects us to our ancestors. The Book of Jasher is being translated, which I am myself editing."

You'll have thought that my lyrics were a pretty poor representation of your wonderful concepts.

"You speak challenging Hebrew. But the overall impression seemed to indicate that you understood the brilliance of my conception."

"Ah, certainly! I endured oppression and mockery while residing in Judengasse."

"But there is worse than oppression--there is inward stagnation of the spiritual life. My idea came to me in Tunis, where the Jews are a little oppressed. You know President Madison appointed me consul of the United States for the city and kingdom of Tunis, one of the most respectable and interesting stations in the regencies of Barbary. I had long desired to visit the country of Dido and Hannibal, trace the field of Zama, and seek out the ruins of Utica,--whose sites I believe I have now successfully established,--but it was my main design to investigate the condition of the Barbary Jews, of whom, you will remember, we have no account later than Benjamin of Tudela's in the thirteenth century. But do not stand--take a chair. Well, I found our brethren--to the number of seven hundred thousand--controlling everything in Barbary, farming the revenue, regulating the coinage, keeping the Dey's jewels and almost his person,--

in short, anything but persecuted, though, of course, the majority were miserably poor. They did not know I was a Jew--though Secretary Monroe recalled me because I was, and it was Monroe's doctrine that Judaism would be an obstacle to the discharge of my functions. Absurd! The Catholic priest was allowed to sprinkle the Consulate with holy water: the barefooted Franciscan received an alms, nor did I fail to acknowledge by a donation the decorated branch sent on Palm Sunday by the Greek Bishop. And as for the slaves, I assure you they were not backward in coming to ask favors. The only people who never came to me were precisely the Jews. I went about among them incognito, so to speak, like Haroun Alraschid among his subjects; hence I was able to see all the evils that will never be eliminated till Israel is again a nation."

"Ah! The advice in your words is wise. The source of the problem is something you have contact with. I have always told them this.

Noah sprang to his feet and stood out with a regal bearing that complemented his large shoulders. Yes, I decided that it would be my responsibility to uplift my people and encourage them to stand high their heads in this era of liberty and awareness.

It will rest on Ararat because it is the Ark of the Covenant and the Deluge.

"True—and like the original Noah, I might create a new universe. I've been in touch with people all across the world. You are the kind of person who will lead thousands of people away from the corrupt tyrannies in Europe and towards the land of the free.

"True--and like the first Noah, I may become the progenitor of a new world. I have communications from the four corners of the earth. You are the type of thousands who will flee from the rotting tyrannies of Europe into the great free republic which I shall direct."

He started to pace the space. Pelosi saw in his dreams vast, black bands of pilgrims coming from all directions.

He hesitantly asked, "But this Grand Island — is it yours?"

"I and a few others who trust in the glorious future of our people have purchased thousands of acres of it."

"Jews?"

Capitalists who understand that we will become the commercial hub of the new world, or the world of the future, say, "No, not Jews."

Pelosi cried out. "And Jews won't accept it? We must visit non-Christians. Jews only invest in Gentile plans; they always construct for others and never for themselves. In every place, it is the same. Oh, poor Israel!"

"It is what I preach. Why administer Barbary for a savage Dey when you can administer Grand Island for yourself? Seven hundred thousand Jews in savage Barbary, and throughout these vast free States not seven thousand. Ah, but they will come; they will come. Ararat will gather its millions."

"But will there be room?"

"The State of New York," replied Noah, impressively, "is the largest in the Union, containing forty-three thousand two hundred and fourteen square miles divided into fifty-five counties and having six thousand and eighty-seven post-towns and cities together with six million acres of cultivated land. The constitution is founded on equality of rights. We recognize no religious differences. In our seven thousand free schools and gymnasia, four hundred thousand children of every religion are being educated. Here in this great and progressive State, the long wandering of my beloved people shall end."

"But Grand Island itself?" murmured Peloni feebly.

"Come here," and Noah unrolled a great map. "See, how nobly it is situated in the Niagara River, near the world-famed Falls, which will supply water-power for our machinery. It is twelve miles long and from three to seven broad, and contains seventeen thousand acres. Lake Erie is two hundred and seventy miles long and borders New York, Pennsylvania, and Ohio, as well as Canada. And see! by navigable streams this great lake is connected with all that wonderful chain of lakes. By short canals, we shall connect with the Illinois and Mississippi, and trade with New Orleans and the Gulf of Mexico. Through the Ontario--see here!--we traffic with Quebec, Montreal, and touch the great Atlantic. The Niagara Falls, as I said, turn our machinery. The fur trade, the lumber trade, all is ours. Our cattle multiply and our lands wave with harvests. We are the center of the world, the capital of the future. And look! See what the _Albany Gazette_ says: 'Here the Hebrews can have their Jerusalem without fearing the legions of Titus. Here they can erect their Temple without dreading the torches of frenzied soldiers. Here they can lay their heads on their pillows at night without fear of mobs, of bigotry and persecution.'"

Pelosi drew a long breath, enraptured by this holy El Dorado, sparkling on the map, amid its tributary lakes and rivers.

"You will see the eighteenth chapter of Isaiah fulfilled," Noah went on. "For what is the 'land shadowing with wings, which is beyond the rivers of Ethiopia,' which shall send messengers to a nation scattered and peeled? What but America, shadowing us with the wings of its eagle? As it is written elsewhere, 'I will bear thee on eagle's wings.' It is true the English Bible translates 'Woe to the land,' but this is a mistranslation. It should be 'Hail to the land!' Also the word '_goumey_' translate as 'bulrushes'--' that sendeth messengers in vessels of bulrushes!' But does not '_goumey_' also mean 'rush, impetus?' And is it not therefore a prophecy of those new steam vessels that are beginning to creep up, one of which has just crossed from England to India? Erelong they will be running between America and all the world. It is the Lord making ready for the easy ingathering of His people. Ay, and along these lakes"--the Prophet's finger swept the map--"will be heard the panting of mighty steam monsters, all making for Ararat. By the way, Ararat lies here," and he indicated a spot of the island opposite Tonawanda on the mainland.

In a lyrical gesture reminiscent of Jehuda Halevi kissing the sacred ground, Peloni knelt and put his lips to the ground.

He asked worried, "There is no one in possession there."

Maybe a few of Iroquois Indians," Noah guessed. However, they won't need to be destroyed like the Hittites, Amorites, and Jebusites were by our predecessors.

Pelosi mumbled, "No?"

"Not. They are our brothers that the King of Assyria has abducted. The Red Indians are the Lost Ten Tribes of Israel, beyond a shadow of a doubt."

Pelosi exclaimed, visibly excited, "What?"

"I'll write a book about it and publish it. Yes, it is our very custom to engage in sacrifices, marriages, divorces, burials, fastings, purifications, and penalties. We also divide tribes into High Priests and engage in wars and victories."

"And after that, I suppose one could stay with them. I want to become settled in Ararat right away."

The great man arched his eyebrows and remarked, "You can hardly settle there till the forest is cleared.

The jungle," echoed Peloni, startled.

"You are shocked, I see. You're a European who is used to prefabricated cities. While you wait, we Americans shift continents and overnight construct Aladdin's palaces. I'll map out the city as soon as I can manage to cover any ground."

Pelosi said, "You haven't been there yet?

"Ah, my dear Peloni. When should I find time to travel to Buffalo,--a busy editor, lawyer, playwright, what not? True, the time that other men give to domestic happiness the President of the Old Bachelors' Club can give to his fellow men. But the slow canal voyage--"

A servant knocked on the door and asked whether Major Noah might see his tailor at this precise moment.

Ah, a good omen, exclaimed the major. The tailor is here to try on my robe as Israel's Governor and Judge.

The man carried a lavish crimson silk robe with ermine trim, which he draped over Noah's stocky frame and marked with chalk and pins where it could be modified to fit more comfortably.

Do you like it, Noah asked, puffing himself up in a regal manner.

Pelosi's unease disappeared. Before these amazing truths, doubt was unthinkable. The Americans were great, I must say.

A servant knocked on the door and asked whether Major Noah might see his tailor at this precise moment.

Ah, a good omen, exclaimed the major. The tailor is here to try on my robe as Israel's Governor and Judge.

The man carried a lavish crimson silk robe with ermine trim, which he draped over Noah's stocky frame and marked with chalk and pins where it could be modified to fit more comfortably.

Do you like it, Noah asked, puffing himself up in a regal manner.

Pelosi's unease disappeared. Before these amazing truths, doubt was unthinkable. The Americans were great, I must say.

"I had to go through our annals," Noah explained, "to find which period of our government we could revive. Kingship was opposed to the sentiment of these States: in the epoch of the Judges, I found my ideal. Indeed, what is the President of the United States but a _Shophet_, a Judge of Israel? Ah, you are looking at that painting of me--I shall have to be done again in my new robes. That elegant creature who hangs beside me is Miss Leesugg, the Hebe of English actresses, as she appeared in my 'She would be a Soldier or the Plains of Chippewa.' There is a caricature of my uncle, Aaron J. Phillips, as the Turkish Commander in my 'Grecian Captive.' Dear me, shall I ever forget how he tumbled off that elephant! Ha! ha! ha! That is Miss Johnson, in my 'Yusef Carmatti, or the Siege of Tripoli.' The black and white is a fancy sketch of 'Marion, or the Hero of Lake George,' a play I wrote for the reopening of the Park Theatre and to celebrate the evacuation of New York by the British in 1783."

The tailor said, "Ah, I was there, Major." "Bullying, that. But there were so many generals and colonels in the house that it was difficult to hear anything."

Fortunately for me, Noah chuckled. "Yes, I requested that they arrive in full uniform to enhance the special event. This brings me to my next point: enjoy this ticket."

Pelosi accepted it and mumbled, "For the play?"

Noah paused and gave him a careful look. But when he saw Peloni's innocent face, his anger-fueled flush subsided. For the inaugural ceremony of Ararat's foundation, he clarified, "No, no."

Pelosi had brilliant black eyes.

Only ticket holders will be allowed entry into the church because there will be a huge crowd.

Pelosi echoed, palely, "Into the church!"

The Judge of Israel impressively responded, "Yes," while adjusting the red robe's elegant folds as he stood before a glass. The Episcopal Church has been kindly loaned to us by our fellow citizens in Buffalo for the event.

"What ritual?" He stumbled as horrifying visions flashed before him and heard the taunting call of "Missionary!" coming from Frankfort.

"The placing of Ararat's foundation stone."

"Building a church from the ground up!" Pelosi wasn't sure why.

"The Major misunderstood him and remarked, "Ah, you see it weird, nursed in the musty lap of Europe. However, in this free country and this enlightenment era, all men are brothers."

But undoubtedly Grand Island should host the laying of the cornerstone.

"It would have been desirable. But so many will wish to be present at this great celebration. Buffalo alone has some thirteen hundred inhabitants. How should we get them across? There are scarcely any boats to be had--and Ararat is twelve miles away. No, no, it is better to hold our ceremony in Buffalo. It is, after all, only symbolism. The cornerstone is already inscribed in Hebrew and English. 'Hear, O Israel, the Lord is our God. Ararat, a City of Refuge for the Jews, founded by Mordecai M. Noah in the month

Tishri, corresponding with September 1825, in the fiftieth year of American Independence."'v

Pelosi's composure was partially restored by the thunderous recitation of the "Shophet" in his crimson and ermine robe.

But when will construction on the actual city start? he questioned.

The "Shophet" made a light hand motion. Just a few days.

But are you certain we can construct there?

"Examine the map. Grand Island is right here, ours! This is where Ararat is located. Everything is as simple as a pikestaff. Speaking of pikestaffs, it could be a good idea to place one on Mount Ararat bearing the Israeli flag."

Pelosi lit a match: "Yes, please allow me to plant it. I'll travel day and night."

The _Shophet_ gently said, "You shall plant it." "Yes, I will make the flag right away. I'll take care of it with the help of the Park Theatre's property manager. Judah's Lion and seven stars."

Before you start the celebration in Buffalo, it will be waving on Grand Island.

Pelosi left with his head in the seven stars, leaving like a lion. Could it be possible that Peloni received the honor of announcing the New Jerusalem?

part 4

The sparse settlement of Buffalo, after the bustle of New York, was peaceful yet a little chilly to the Ghetto-bred poet, with his rapid mind, unaccustomed to the slow processes of nature. Buffalo was still partially in and partially out of mother earth with its muddy, unpaved streets and large trees, up which squirrel and chipmunk ran. Man's artifice ruled in the high street with its stores and inns, some of which were even made of brick, but in the byways now and then a primitive log cabin broke the line of frame cottages, and in the suburbs cows and pigs wandered around carelessly. It served as a reminder of everything that needed to be accomplished in Ararat before a Temple could serve as a beacon of righteousness for the wandering peoples. Peloni, though, felt encouraged and warmed at the flame when he realized that it had only been twelve years since the British and Indians had destroyed the barely-born village during the war. His heart grew into new poetry when he realized that while the locals were enthralled by Ararat and the church celebration, other topics of conversation included the Erie Canal, the hanging of the three Thayers, and General Lafayette's most recent visit to the Eagle Tavern.

It was indeed an auspicious moment for Noah's scheme. All eyes were turned on the coming celebration of the opening of the great canal, to be the terminus of which Buffalo had fought victoriously against Black Rock. Golden visions of the future gleamed almost tangibly, and amid the general magnificence Noah's ornate dream took on equal solidity. Endless capital would be directed into the neighborhood of Buffalo--for Ararat was only twelve miles away. Besides, all the great men of Buffalo--and there were many--had been honored with elaborate cards of invitation to the grand ceremony of the foundation stone. A few old Baptist farmers were surly about the threatened vast Jewish immigration, but the majority proclaimed with righteous warmth that the glorious American Constitution welcomed all creeds and that there was money in it.

Pelosi looked about for a Jew to guide him but could find none. Finally, a Seneca Indian from the camp just below Buffalo undertook to look for the spot. It was with a strange thrill that Peloni's eyes rested for the first time on a red

Indian. Was this indeed a long-lost brother of his? He cried "Shalom Aleichem" in Hebrew, but the Indian, despite Noah's theories, did not seem to understand. Ultimately the dialogue was carried on in the few words of broken English that the Indian had picked up from the trappers, and in the gesture language, in which, with his genius for all languages, Peloni was soon at home. And in truth, he did find at heart some subtle sympathy with this copper-colored savage which was not called out by the busy citizens of Buffalo. On a sunlit morning, bearing his flagstaff with the flag wrapped around it, a blanket, and a little store of provisions for camping out overnight, Peloni slipped into the birch canoe and the Indian paddled off. For miles, they glided in silence along the sparkling Niagara, lone denizens of a lonely world.

Suddenly Peloni thought of the _Judengasse_ of Frankfort, and for a moment it seemed to him that he must be dreaming. What! a few short months ago he was selling prayer books and phylacteries in the shadow of the old high-gabled houses, and now, in a virgin district of the New World, in company with a half-naked red Indian, he was going to plant the flag of Judah on an island forest and to found the New Jerusalem. What would they say, his old friends, if they could see him now? And he--the _Possemacher_--what winged jest would he let fly? A perception of the monstrous fantasy of the thing stole on poor Peloni. Was he, perhaps, dreaming after all? No, there was the Niagara River, the village of Black Rock on his right hand, and on the other side of the gorge the lively Fort Erie and the poplar-fringed Canadian shore, and there too--on the map, Noah had given him--Ararat lay waiting.

The Indian paddled imperturbably, throwing back the sparkling water with a soft, soothing sound. Pelosi lapsed into more pleasurable reflections. How beautiful was this great free place of sun and wind, of water and forest, after the noisome Jew street! He was not dreaming, nor--thank God!--was Noah. Strange, indeed, that thus should deliverance for Israel be wrought; yet what was Israel's history but a series of miracles? And his--Peloni's--humble hand was to plant the flag that had lain folded and inglorious these twenty centuries!

A large, forested, dark purple mass with a ring of deep orange along the low coastline rose to greet them as they passed past a few small islands that had been properly depicted on the chart.

This was Grand Island.

Pelosi prayed in a low voice.

The canoe smoothly rounded the island, staying on the American side, following the map that Noah had marked. A low explosion could be heard as they passed a third tiny island.

Whoa, what's that? Pelosi's face was inquisitive.

The Indian smiled. "Not go many miles farther," he indicated. "The Rapids soon. Then--whizz! The big jump! Niagara. Dead."

Fortunately, Ararat was due much sooner than Niagara. As they drew near the fourth of the little islands, which lay betwixt Grand Island and the mainland of the States, and saw the Tonawanda Creek emptying itself into the river, Peloni signed to the Indian to land; for it was here that Ararat was to arise.

The landing was easy, the river here being shallow and the bank low. The beauty of the spot, as it lay wild and fresh from God's hand in the golden sunlight, moved Peloni to tears. The Indian, who seemed curious as to his movements and willing to share his mid-day meal, tied his canoe to a basswood tree and followed the standard-bearer. There was a glorious medley of leafy life--elm, oak, maple, linden, pine, wild cherry, wild plum--which Peloni could only rejoice in without differentiating it by names; and as the oddly assorted couple walked through the sun-dappled glades they startled a world of scurrying animal life--snipe and plover and partridges and singing-birds, squirrels and rabbits and even deer, that frisked and fluttered unprescient of the New Jerusalem that menaced their immemorial inheritance. The joy of city-building had begun at last to dawn on Peloni, the immense pleasure to the human will of beginning afresh, of shaking off the pressure of the ages, of inscribing free ideas on the plastic universe. As he wandered at random in search of a suitable spot on which to plant the flagstaff, the romance of this great American world thrilled him, of this vast continent won acre by acre from nature and the savage, covering itself with splendid cities; a retrospective sympathy with the citizens of Buffalo and their coming canal warmed his breast.

He then heard screaming and looked up to see two odd, enormous birds perched on a burned-out pine.

Eagles, the terse Indian replied.

"Eagles!" Pelosi suddenly remembered what Noah had said, and his heart jumped. "Here, beneath their wings, our flag will be raised. Israel is that blasted tree that will once more blossom."

He dug the pole into the earth. A breeze caught the flag, and the folds flew out, and the Lion of Judah and the seven stars flapped in the face of an inattentive universe. Pelosi intoned the Hebrew benediction, closing his eyes in pious ecstasy. "Blessed art Thou, O Lord our God, who hast kept us alive, and preserved us, and enabled us to reach this day!"

As he opened his eyes, he noticed a large cloud of shimmering spray rising far over the Island in the distance, inside which rainbows netted and entangled themselves in an unfathomable dreamlike beauty. Over the boom of the rapids, at the same time, his ear heard the first hints of another, mightier, and more beautiful roar.

The Indian whispered, "Niagara."

Peloni, though, had his gaze firmly fixated on the heavenly spectacle.

He sneered, "The Shechinah!" The heavenly presence that was present in the Tabernacle and Solomon's Temple has finally made its way back to Ararat.

part 5.

The Court House and the Terrace facing the lake both blasted cannons to welcome the sunny September dawn and to remind Buffalo residents that the Messianic day had come. But they didn't require reminding. The elite had dressed in their finest attire, and Masonic regalia and military insignia had been set up. St. Paul's Church was protected by troops who kept the thronging mob at bay.

To the sound of patriotic American airs, the opening act of the grand historical play "Mordecai Manuel Noah; or, The Redemption of Israel" concluded gloriously. This stage pageant marshaller was honored by the procession that left the Lodge at eleven and proceeded through the main streets.

ORDER OF PROCESSION

Grand Marshal, Col. Potter, on horseback.

Music.

Military.

Citizens.

Civil Officers.

State Officers in Uniform.

President and Trustees of the Corporation.

Tyler.
Stewards.
Entered Apprentices.
Fellow Crafts.
Master Masons.
Senior and Junior Deacons.
Secretary and Treasurer.
Senior and Junior Wardens.
Master of Lodges.
Past Masters.
Rev. Clergy.
Stewards, with corn, wine, and oil.
, Principal Architect, |
Globe | with square, level, | globe, and plumb. ,
Bible.
Square and Compass, borne by a Master Mason.
The Judge of Israel
In black, wearing the judicial robes of crimson silk, trimmed
with ermine, and a richly embossed golden
medal suspended from the neck.
A Master Mason.
Royal Arch Masons.
Knights Templars.

At the church door, there was a halt. The troops parted to right and left, the pageant passed through into the crowded church, gay with the summer dresses of the ladies, the band played the grand march from "Judas Maccabæus," the organ pealed out the "Jubilate." On the communion table lay the cornerstone of Ararat!

The morning service was read by the Rev. Mr. Searle in full canonicals; the choir sang "Before Jehovah's Awful Throne"; then came a special prayer for Ararat, and passages from Jeremiah, Zephaniah, and the Psalms, charged with divine promises and consolations for the long-suffering of Israel, idyllic pictures of the Messianic future, symbolized by the silver cups with wine, corn, and oil, that lay on the corner-stone. At last arose, with that crimson silk robe trimmed with ermine thrown over his stately black attire, and with the richly embossed golden medal hanging from his neck--the Master of the Show, the Dramatist of the Real, the Humorist without a sense of Humour, the Dreamer of the Ghetto and American Man of Action, the Governor and Judge of Israel, the _Shophet_,--in brief, Mordecai Manuel Noah. He delivered a great discourse on the history of Israel and its present reorganization, which filled more than five columns of the newspapers, and was heard with solemn attention by the crowded Christian audience. Save a few Indians and his secretary, not a single Jew was present to hold in check the orator's oriental imagination. Then the glittering procession filed back to the Lodge, and the brethren and the military dined joyously at the Eagle Tavern, and Noah's wit and humor returned for the after-dinner speech. He withdrew early to write a full account of the proceedings for the _Buffalo Patriot Extra_.

The historic day of Israel's restoration was concluded by a salvo of twenty-four guns.

part 6.

Pelosi was waiting for the arrival of the island's Ruler while on his island. He vaguely recalled the cannonade that began and ended the church's chancel's laying of the foundation stone, and he anticipated Noah by the next day at the latest. However, Noah was absent the following day. Although Peloni's Indian guide had vanished and he was now a prisoner, he continued to eat his leftover corn and drink from the river because he could see the wigwams of another Indian encampment across the river, and occasionally a group of them would pass by in a large canoe. Despite this, Peloni had no fear of starvation. While still hungry On this first day, his senses were mouthwatering. The poet in him was enthralled by the allure of this new life, which included the chance to experience the animal kingdom's fraternity, sleep under the stars in a vast night, and witness the sunrise's silent, passionate beauty as it ripened to the sound of birds.

On the second day, his eyes were gladdened by the oncoming of a boat rowed by two whites. They proved to be a stone mason and his man, and they bore provisions, a letter, and newspapers from Noah:--

"MY DEAR PELONI:

"A hurried line to report a glorious success, thank Heaven! A finer day and more general satisfaction have not been known on any similar occasion. All the dignity and talent of the neighborhood for miles were present. I hear that a vast concourse also assembled at Tonawanda, expecting that the ceremonies would be at Grand Island, but that many of them came up in carriages in time to hear my Inaugural Speech. You will see that the newspapers, especially the _Buffalo Patriot Extra_, have reported me fully, showing how they realize the importance of this world-stirring episode in Israel's history. Their comments, too, are for the most part highly sympathetic. Of course the _New York Herald_ will sneer; but then Bennett was once in my employ on the _Courier and Enquirer_. They tell me that you duly set out to plant the flag of Judah, and I assume it is now by God's grace waving over Ararat. Heaven bless you! my heart is too full for words. I had hoped to find time today to behold the sublime spectacle myself, but urgent legal business calls me back to New York. But I am resolved to start the city without delay, and the bearers of this have my plan for a little monument of brick and wood with the simple inscription--‘ Ararat founded by Mordecai Manuel Noah, 1825’--from the summit of which the flag can wave. I leave you to superintend the same and take any measures you please to promote the growth of the city and to receive, as my representative, the inflowing immigrants from the Ghettos of the world. I appoint you, moreover, Keeper of the Records. To you shall be given to write the new Book of the Chronicles of Israel. My friend Mr. Smith, one of the proprietors of the island, will communicate with you on behalf of the Shareholders, as the occasion arises. Expect me shortly (perhaps with my bride, for I am entering into holy wedlock with the most amiable and beautiful of her sex) and meantime receives my blessing.

"MORDECAI MANUEL NOAH, Judge of Israel,

"_pro_ A.B. SEIXAS, Secr. _pro tem._"

While the little monument was building, and the men were coming to and fro in boats, Peloni made friends with the Indians, the smoke-wreaths of whose lodges hovered across the river, and he picked up a little of their language. Also, he explored his island, drawn by the crescendo roar of Niagara. It was at Burnt Island Bay that he had his first if the distant, view of the Falls themselves. The rapids, gurgling and plunging with foam and swirl and eddy, quickened his blood, but cataracts disappointed him, after that rainbow glimpse of the upper spray, and it was not till he got himself landed on the Canadian shore and saw the monstrous rush of the vast tameless flood toward the great leap that he felt the presence and the power that were to be with him for the rest of his days. The bend of the Horse-Shoe was hidden by a white spray mountain that rose above its topmost waters, as they hurled themselves from green solidity to creamy mist. And as he looked, lo! the enchanting rainbows twinkled again, and he had a sense as of the smile of God, of the love of that awful, unfathomable Being, eternally persistent, while the generations rise and fall like vaporous spray.

The tide was low and, drawn by an irresistible fascination, he adventured down among the rocks near the foot of the Fall. But a tingling storm of spray smote him half blind and wholly breathless, and all he could see was a monstrous misty Brocken spirit upreared, and in his ears were a thousand thunders. A wild elemental passion swelled and lifted him. Yes, Force, Force, was the secret of things: the vast primal energies that sent the stars shining and the seas roaring. Force, Life, Strength, that was what Israel needed. It had grown anæmic, slouching along its airless _Judengassen_. Oh, to fight, to fight, like the warriors who went out against the Greeks, who defended the Holy City against the Romans. "For the Lord is a Man of War." And he shouted the cry of David, "Blessed be the Lord, my Rock, who teacheth my hands to war, and my fingers to fight." But he stopped, smitten by an ironic memory. This very blessing was uttered every Sabbath twilight, in every Ghetto, by every bloodless worshipper, to a melancholy despairing melody, in the lightless dusk of the synagogues.

The monument was speedily erected and, being hollow, proved useful for Peloni to sleep in, as the October nights grew chilly. And thus Peloni lived, a latter-day Crusoe. He had now procured fishing tackle and grew dexterous in luring black bass and perch and whitefish from the river. Also, he had found out what berries he might eat. Occasionally a boat would sell him cornmeal from Buffalo, but his savings were melting away and he preferred to forage for himself, relishing the wild flavor of uncivilized living. He even wished it were possible to eat the birds or the rabbits he could have killed: but as various points of Jewish law forbade such diet, there was no use in buying a musket or a bow and arrow. So his relations with the animal world remained purely amicable. The robins and bluebirds and thrushes sang for him. The woodpeckers tapped on his monument to wake him in the morning. The blue jays screamed without wrath, and the partridges drummed unmartially. The squirrels frolicked with him, and the rabbits lost their shyness. One would have said these were the Lost Ten Tribes he had found.

Instead of being the Keeper of the Records, Peloni had changed to being the Keeper of Noah's Ark.

part 7.

Winter arrived, but little was left to be written down except the enchantment of the muffled white world with its blue shadows, wonderful ice friezes, and stalactites. On the rocks, large icicles gleamed, revealing all the colors below. On his monument, Peloni knelt over a burning log as he was covered by his blanket.

It felt quite solitary. Neither Noah nor Smith nor any other Jewish or even Indian traveler to the New Jerusalem had contacted him.

and the stock of winter provisions had exhausted his little hoard of the coin. The old despair began to twine around him like some serpent of ice. As he listened in such moods to the distant thunder of Niagara--which waxed louder as the air grew heavier, till it quite dominated the ever-present rumble of the rapids--the sound took on endless meanings to his feverish brain. Now it was no longer the voice of the Eternal Being, it was the endless plaint of Israel beseeching the deaf heaven, the roar of prayer from some measureless synagogue; now it was the raucous voice of persecution, the dull bestial roar of malicious multitudes; and again it was the voice of the whole earth, groaning and travailing. And the horror of it was that it would not stop. It dropped on his brain, this falling water, as on the prisoners in the mediæval torture chamber. Could no one stop this turning wheel of the world, jar it grindingly to a standstill?

Spring wore slowly round again. The icicles melted, the friezes dripped away, the fantastic mufflers slipped from the trees, the young buds peeped out and the young birds sang. The river flowed uncurdled, the cataracts fell unclogged.

In Peloni's breast alone the ice did not melt: no new sap stirred in his veins. The very rainbows on the leaping mist were now only reminders of the Biblical promise that the world would go on forever; forever the wheel would turn, and Israel wander homeless.

And at last one sunny day a b, oat arrived with a message from the Master. Alas! even Noah had abandoned Ararat. "I am beginning to see," he wrote, "that our only hope is intestine. Zion alone has magnetism for the Jew. The great war against Gog prophesied in Ezekiel will be in Palestine. Gog is Russia, and the Russians are the descendants of the joint colony of Meshech and Tubal and the little horn of Daniel. Russia in an attempt to wrest India and Turkey from the English and the Turks will make the Holy Land the theatre of a terrible conflict. But yet in the end in Jerusalem shall we reërect Solomon's Temple. The ports of the Mediterranean will be again open to the busy hum of commerce; the fields will again bear the fruitful harvest, and Christians and Jew will together, on Mount Zion, raise their voices in praise of Him whose covenant with Abraham was to endure forever, in whose seed all the nations of the earth are to be blessed. This is our destiny."

PelPelosindered automatically to the apex of the island at Burnt Ship Bay, ad stood gazing meaninglessly at the fragments of the sunken ships. Before he raced the rapids, frenziedly anxious for the great leap. Even so, he thought, had Noah and he dreamed Israel would haste to Ararat. And Niagara maintained its mocking roar--its roar of gigantic laughter.

Reërect Solomon's Temple in Palestine! A ruined country to regenerate a ruined people! Land belonging to the Turks, the center of the fanaticisms of three religions and countless sects! A soil which even to Noah was the destined theatre of world-shaking war!

As he lifted his swimming eyes he saw to his astonishment that he was no longer alone. A tall majestic figure stood gazing at him: a grave, sorrowful Indian, feathered and tufted, habited only in buckskin leggings and girdled by a belt of wampum. A musket in his hand showed he had been hunting, and a canoe Peloni now saw tethered to the bank indicated he was going back to his lodge. Pelosi knew from his talks with the Tonawanda Indians opposite Ararat that this was Red Jacket, the famous chief of the Iroquois, the ancient lords of the soil. Pelosi tendered the salute due to the royalty stamped on the man. Red Jacket ceremoniously acknowledged the obeisance. Then they gazed silently at each other, the puny, stooping scholar from the German Ghetto, and the stalwart, kingly savage.

What nation are you, Red Jacket demanded imperiously, "that you never create a city like the other white men, nor even a camp like my people, but only erect a monument?"

We are a people who construct for others, Peloni retorted in his finest Iroquois.

"Then, I would have you construct for my people. As a result, these white men push us further and further away until there is nothing except "—and he made a powerful gesture that suggested being swept down the river and into the rushing rapids' jaws. However, I believe I have heard of a plan for your people to establish a large metropolis here through a large pow-wow of your chiefs in a church.

It is already dead at birth, Peloni added.

"Strange," mused Red Jacket. "Scarce twenty summers ago Joseph Elliott came here to plan out his city on a soil that was not his, and lo! this Buffalo rises already mighty and menacing. Tomorrow it will be at my wigwam door--and we"--another gesture, hopeless, yet full of regal dignity, rounded off the sentence.

And in that instant, it was borne in upon Peloni that they were indeed brothers: the Jew who stood for the world that could not be born again, and the Red Indian who stood for the world that must pass away. Yes, they were both doomed. Israel had been too bent and broken by the long dispersion and the long persecution: the spring was snapped; he could not recover. He had been too long the pliant protégé of kings and popes: he had prayed too many centuries in too many countries for the simultaneous welfare of too many governments, to be capable of realizing that government of his own for which he likewise prayed. This pious patience--this rejection of the burden on to the shoulders of Messiah and Miracle--was it more than the veil of unconscious impotence? Ah, better sweep oneself away than endure the long ignominy. And Niagara laughed on.

He requested, "May I have the honor of crossing in your canoe?"

Red Jacket asked, "You're not afraid?" There are deadly rapids here.

Afraid! Pelosi thought his internal laughter matched Niagara's.

When he got to the mainland, he made straight for the Fall. He was on the American side, and he paused on the sward, on the very brink of the tameless cataract, that had for immemorial ages been driving itself backward by eating away its rock. His fascinated eyes watched the curious smooth, purring slide of the vast mass of green water over the sharp edges, unending, unresting, the eternal revolution of a maddening, imperturbable wheel. O that blind wheel, turning, turning, while the generations waxed and waned, one succeeding the other without haste or rest or the possibility of pause: creatures of meaningless majesty, shadows of shadows, dreaming of love and justice, and fading into the kindred mist, while this solid green cataract roared and raced through æons innumerable, stable as the stars, thundering in majestic meaninglessness. And suddenly he threw himself into its remorseless whirl and was sucked down into the monstrous chaos of seething waters and whirled and hurled amid the rocks, battered and shapeless, but still holding Noah's letter in his convulsively clinched hand, while the rainbowed spray leaped impassively heavenward.

Nobody who copies the inscription on the cornerstone of Ararat dreams that it is the gravestone of Peloni, and it is located inside the Buffalo Historical Society's rooms.

Buffalo, the Queen City of the Empire State, sits thronged amid her waterways, with the world's commerce at her feet, while the very monument in Ararat has withered away. The Christian railroad monarchs depart from their palaces made of Medina sandstone in their opulent yachts, which are steam-powered rather than made of bulrushes, as predicted by Mordecai Manuel Noah,

Governor, and Judge of Israel.

Printed by Libri Plureos GmbH in Hamburg, Germany